B O O K O F

CUCUMBERS, MELONS & SQUASH

NATIONAL **Gardening** ASSOCIATION

BOOK OF

CUCUMBERS, MELONS & SQUASH

Edited by the staff of the
National Gardening magazine

ILLUSTRATIONS BY
ELAYNE SEARS & LYN SEVERANCE

VILLARD BOOKS ▪ NEW YORK ▪ 1987

Library of Congress Catalogue
Card Number: 86-40341

ISBN 0-394-74988-X

Designed by Joel Avirom

Manufactured in the United States of America
9 8 7 6 5 4 3 2
Revised Edition

CONTENTS

BOOK OF

CUCUMBERS, MELONS & SQUASH

VINE CROPS

Cucumbers — The Cool Ones

For a heat-loving plant, the cucumber certainly has all the connotations of coolness attached to it. Considering that it originated in the hot, dry climates of Asia and Africa, we can understand how its crisp, white flesh must have seemed refreshing. Sliced cucumbers are still recommended to soothe hot, tired eyelids and for skin irritations. And there's nothing like sliced cucumbers in a summer salad to beat the heat.

Today, there are many cucumber varieties—picklers, slicers, gherkins, white cucumbers, bush, and midget cukes. The most interesting hybrid to come along in quite a while

is the "burpless" cucumber, guaranteed not to cause "social embarrassment."

The art of pickling and preserving cucumbers is centuries old. You can pickle or preserve any small cucumber. Picklers also taste very good right off the vine, so feel free to experiment with different varieties, regardless of how you intend to eat them. Also, remember to plant some dill seed early in the spring, so you'll be all set for pickling when those first young cucumbers are ready.

The two major varieties are:

Picklers—growing time is fifty-three to sixty days—are smallish, often warty, green, used for small, sweet pickles or large dills. They can also be eaten fresh. A good pickler is *Wisconsin SMR 18*.

Slicers—growing time is fifty-eight to sixty-five days—are 5- to 8-inch cylindrical cucumbers, used for slicing and serving fresh, but they can be pickled. Skin can be solid-colored or white-spined (striped). *Marketmore 70* is an old favorite.

There are also the lemon, serpent, white, burpless, and bush cucumbers available for you to try. Check for them in seed catalogs or at a garden store.

Squashes and Pumpkins—The All-Americans

Each of the different varieties—summer squashes, winter squashes, and pumpkins—has a different length growing season, which makes them easy to tell apart. Summer squashes—zucchini, patty pans, and cocozelles—all take a relatively short time from planting until harvest. Winter squashes take longer to mature, and pumpkins require the longest growing season of all. Plant them all at the same time and you can have different varieties ready to harvest from midsummer up to the first frost.

Sometimes there is confusion over what's a squash and what's really a pumpkin. When we refer to pumpkins, we mean only the round, orange vegetables raised for Halloween and used in making pies.

For many, Thanksgiving dinner just wouldn't be complete without winter squash. Winter squashes originated in Central America, and they were North American Indian specialties long before the Pilgrims ever stepped off the *Mayflower*.

Big, gnarly, bluish-gray *Blue Hubbard* is a favorite of many gardeners. (Smaller families may prefer *Sweet Mama*—it looks and tastes like a small Hubbard.) *Waltham Butternut* is another flavorful variety, and *Table Queen* acorn squash does well in most gardens.

As for summer squash, try to choose varieties that produce very early and are resistant to disease. Most zucchini and straight-neck varieties available these days are dependable producers. Zucchini are green and straight-neck are yellow. Cocozelle and patty pan are two other varieties of summer squash that are as interesting to look at as they are to eat.

Small Sugar pumpkins are good for pies, and *Big Max* for prize-winning jack o'lanterns.

Melons — The Essence of Summer

If anything says "summer," it's a bright red, juicy wedge of chilled watermelon on a hot, sunny afternoon. Maybe you have always considered melons as fruit, but they are also vegetables because they are members of the vine crop (cucurbit) family. But because, technically, the word "fruit" means any ripe, seed-containing growth from a flowering plant, melons can be correctly referred to as either fruit or vegetable.

There is also some confusion about the terms *cantaloupe* and *muskmelon*. A cantaloupe is actually a small, hard-skinned melon which originated in Italy but isn't grown much in America. What we commonly call a cantaloupe in this country is more correctly referred to as a

muskmelon. The confusion arises because the two names have come to mean exactly the same thing in this country. Seed companies, grocers, and local growers use the terms interchangeably.

How All Vine Crops Grow

Vine crop seeds and plants are extremely tender. They don't tolerate frosts at all, and they need both warm weather and lots of sunshine.

Once the seeds are planted, they'll sprout (germinate) in seven days to two weeks, depending on the variety.

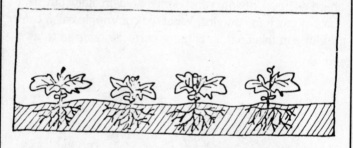

In order to do this, the seeds need moisture and warmth.

Soon after the seeds have germinated, they'll send up their first leaves. The vines will lengthen quickly from this point on, putting on new leaf growth the entire time.

While the vines spread, the roots below develop an extensive but fairly shallow network in the top 12 inches of the soil. There is one strong taproot that grows as deep as 2 to 3 feet, but most of the food, moisture, and air is delivered by the many branching offshoots just below the soil surface.

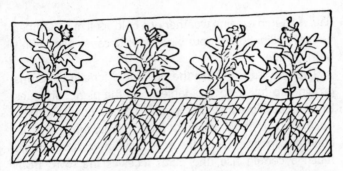

Tendrils will eventually form on the vines to anchor them. These tendrils can wind tightly around fences, trellises, or even other vegetables for support.

Flowers appear after about three weeks of initial growth. The first blossoms that appear are usually male. They produce pollen. About a week later, the fruit-producing female blossoms will appear. You can tell the blossoms apart because the females have tiny fruit at their base.

Once both the brightly colored male and female blossoms appear on the vine, bees transfer the pollen from the males to the females. Each flower lives for only half a

day. A stretch of rainy weather or a cold spell may hamper natural pollination of your vine crops because bees won't be so active.

The tiny fruits behind the pollinated female blossoms grown into full-sized vegetables, and the plant continues to produce blossoms. The plant's natural goal is to produce seeds that will produce more plants, thus perpetuating the species. Once the seeds within each vegetable reach a certain size, the plant receives the word from Mother Nature to stop producing more female flowers for more fruit. The plant's job is done.

The Facts of Life

There are some pretty tall tales about the freak results of cross-pollination between cucumbers and melons, pumpkins and squash. These old wives' tales need clearing up.

First of all, the whole notion of mixed breeding of melons or squash only matters if you intend to save seed from one year for the next. Vine crops will never show the results of cross-pollination in the first season. It's what the bees were up to the previous year that can cause strange-looking vegetables. That's why seed companies isolate vine crops very strictly—if two crops' blossoms mix this year, it will show up in the seed you buy for next year.

Sometimes, even with the most careful controls, the commercial seed that's available may have one or two "weirdo" seeds mixed in with it, and you may raise a strange-looking zucchini. But it isn't because of anything that happened in your own garden.

Now, if you do intend to save seed from your pumpkins or squash to plant next year, you should understand that

only some vine crops are able to cross with one another. Keep it straight with this formula: "Each species keeps to its own kind." Summer squash will cross with each other, but not with cucumbers. Cucumbers will interbreed, but won't cross with anything else. Muskmelons will cross with each other, but not with watermelons. Winter squash, summer squash, and pumpkins are closely related, and they may cross among themselves. Gourds are a species unto themselves, for the most part, but some will cross with summer squash.

If you want to grow two kinds of summer squash—say, zucchini and cocozelle—and you plan to save the seed, plant them at least 100 feet apart to prevent the bees from traveling back forth, mixing pollens. It's probably safest to stick with commercially grown, disease-resistant seed for your main yield, and to plant home-grown seeds only for fun.

A point on hybrids: If you plant a hybrid, even a commercially grown variety, don't save the seed. Hybrids don't reproduce themselves exactly. Instead, they revert back to the traits of their parent plants, and are usually inferior in quality.

Vine Vocabulary

CUCURBITS	The family of plants that includes cucumbers, melons, squashes, pumpkins, and gourds.
CULTIVATION	The stirring up to the top ¼ to ½ inch of garden soil to kill weeds and aerate the soil.
DRILL	Row of seeds spaced at fixed intervals at planting.
GYNECIOUS	Having only female flowers on the vine, requiring the presence of male flowers on an accompanying plant for pollination.
HILL	Group of plants or seeds usually arranged in a circle on level ground.
MONOECIOUS	Having both male and female flowers on the same vine.
MOUND	Raised soil used for planting in wet areas or in heavy clay soil; usually isolated on one crop or hill.
MULCH	Protective covering laid on the garden soil around plants and in walkways to retain moisture and prevent weeds. Can be black plastic or organic material such as leaves, compost, or newsprint.

NETTING	Crisscrossed pattern on the skin of muskmelons that becomes more and more pronounced as the fruit ripens.
RIBBING	The series of contours along the outer skin of a melon, pumpkin, or squash. Some varieties have ribbing, some don't.
SLIP	The crack that appears in a melon stem where it attaches to the fruit; indicates ripeness.

SPINES	The wartlike bumps on gherkins and pickling cucumbers; these hold protective needles that deter·pests.
TRANSPLANTS	Young plants initially grown indoors, then planted in the garden when it's warm enough for them to survive.
TRELLIS	Supporting structure for climbing vines and vegetables. Used to save garden space and to keep produce dry and clean.

The Name Game

Some of the names within the vine crop family are so curious, we thought you'd be interested in a bit of background:

CANTALOUPE	Melon variety named for Cantelupo, a castle in Italy, near Rome, where this variety was first grown after it was imported from Armenia.
COCOZELLE	A summer squash variety; Italian variation of the word *cucuzza*, meaning squash.
GHERKIN	Germans named this burrlike cucumber that originated in the West Indies. The German word for cucumber is *gurke*, hence gherkin.
PATTY PAN	The fluted rind of this summer squash caused it to be named for the small pans used for baking "patties"—rounded vegetable, meat, or fish cakes. Probably English in origin.
PUMPKIN	This word is derived from many variations on *Pepo*, the species of some pumpkins. It went from the Latin word *pepo* to *pepon* to *popon* to *pompon* to *pumpkin*—all meaning "a kind of melon."

SQUASH	This is a shortened version of as-kuta-squash, from the Narraganset Indians in this country. It's somewhat misleading, since the literal translation is "vegetables eaten green."
ZUCCHINI	This again is Italian, from their word for gourd, *zucca*; zucchini is the diminutive, meaning "little gourds." Zucchini do taste best when harvested young.

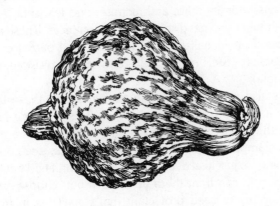

GETTING STARTED

Seed Know-how

When it's time for you to choose seeds, either at a garden center or from a seed catalog, check with a gardening neighbor or your local cooperative extension service agent for advice on which varieties do best in your area. The seed companies have been busy developing strains that are resistant to such vine crop problems as mildews, mosaic, scab, anthracnose, and leaf spot, and you should try to get disease-resistant varieties. These are indicated by capitalized initials on the seed packet or in the catalog. (SMR means scab- and mosaic-resistant, for example).

It's also smart to start with treated seeds, those that have a powdery fungicide on them. This fungicide protects the seeds from rotting before they germinate and from damping off, a fungus disease that causes young seedlings to just keel over and die. If you can't find treated seeds, you can treat them yourself, if you choose, with an all-purpose seed protectant that's available in most garden stores. Be sure to follow the directions.

If you're interested in trying some seeds of the latest hybrids now available in the marketplace, great! But also plant some of the old standbys that you are sure will produce well in your area, in case the others aren't well-adapted. It's fun to see how a few white or all-female cucumbers fare in your garden; however, don't depend entirely on these novelty varieties.

If you're short of space, the bush, or dwarf, varieties are real space-savers.

Garden Planning

Reserve a sunny, well-drained spot for your vine crops, preferable one with a slight slope to the south. Sunny means at least eight hours of full sun every day.

The amount of space you allow depends on how many plants you and your family want, and whether or not you plan to support the vines with trellises or fences. Start off small if you've never grown vine crops before. Cucumbers and all summer squash are especially heavy yielders. A good rule of thumb is one or two hills maximum for each person in the household, and that may still be too much. Of course, if you intend to preserve or store much of the harvest, plant more.

Grow more than one variety. Planting a few that mature early and some later ones will extend the harvest and avoid a sudden overdose of ripe squash or cucumbers. You can stagger your plantings to have continual harvests and to avoid losing an entire crop if weather or disease problems hit. Divide seed packets up with your friends—take a few seeds and pass them on. Believe us, you probably don't need to grow all the vine crop seeds contained in a packet.

Some varieties spread more than others. Keep this in mind as you plan your garden. If you plan to limit the space with supports, leave a walkway wide enough for you to cultivate by hand or machine. If you intend to let the vines run freely, beware . . . some need lots of room. One place to plant vine crops is at the edge of the garden, so the vines can spread over the lawn rather than in among your other vegetables, but this makes is impossible to keep the grass mowed in that area.

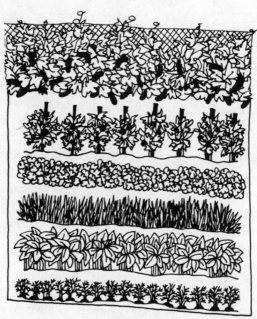

When to Plant

You must wait until all danger of frost is past, unless you provide some protection for sensitive vine crops. These plants shouldn't go into the garden until after the average last frost date, when the soil has really warmed up.

Your local weather bureau or county extension agent can tell you when the average last frost date is expected in your area.

Prep Talk—Soil

Vine crops may be very particular when it comes to their place in the garden, but they are quite flexible when it comes to the soil itself. With a little help from you, they'll flourish in sandy soil, clay soil, or just about anything in between.

It's up to you to till or spade the soil several times before planting day. The first time should be the deepest, to a depth of 6 to 8 inches. Improve the texture of your soil by working in plenty of organic matter at that time. This can be old leaves, hay, grass clippings, compost, or even organic kitchen garbage. The more organic matter you add to your soil, the more food you provide for the earthworms and soil organisms within it. They, in turn, break down the organic matter into humus, a nutrient-rich substance. Humus is the garden miracle worker—it will transform problem soils into productive soils.

If your soil is so sandy that it just doesn't hold moisture, humus binds the sandy particles together to create a more spongelike texture.

On the other hand, if you're plagued by clay soil that either never dries out or bakes as hard as concrete when

it does dry, humus wedges itself between the clay particles. This allows air to circulate and water to seep down
through the soil naturally, making the soil a fine growing
medium.

By adding organic matter to the soil, and by loosening
the top 6 to 8 inches, you make it easy for plant roots to
expand and draw air, water, and nutrients to the rest of
the plant. Result? Healthy, delicious vegetables.

After the initial deep tilling or spading a week to two
before planting, stir up the top 2 to 3 inches of soil every
few days, using an iron garden rake, hoe, cultivating tool,
or tiller. Every time you disrupt the soil section, you bring
hundreds of tiny weed seeds out into the open, where
they die. The more you work the soil, the less weeding
you'll have to do later. This alone should inspire you to
go out often for a soil-prep session.

pH

Most vegetables grow best in soil that is slightly acid, and
vine crops are no exception. You can measure your soil's
acidity or alkalinity by determining its pH with a soil test.
pH is measured on a scale of 0 (the most acid) to 14 (the
most alkaline), with 7 indicating neutral. Any reading above
7 is considered alkaline, or sweet; anything below is acid.
The further the reading is from neutral 7, the greater the
degree of acidity or alkalinity. A pH range of 6.0 to 6.8
—slightly on the acid side—is best for the home garden.

You should check your soil pH every couple of years.
Do this by sending a soil sample to your local cooperative
extension service, if they do tests, or test your own soil
by using an inexpensive soil-testing kit, available at most
garden centers.

If the test results indicate that your soil pH is too high or too low, add lime to raise the pH or sulphur to lower it. Your soil test report or the information with your kit will tell you how to determine appropriate amounts to add.

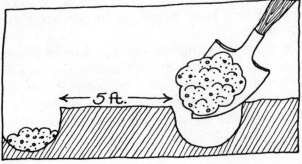

Hearty Appetites — Fertilizer

Planting day is the time to provide your vine crops with a hefty dose of feed to start them growing quickly. It doesn't pay to spread the fertilizer widely, since the plants will be spaced at fairly good intervals and will use only what's directly around their roots. They'll make good use of the manure or fertilizer placed directly in the furrow or hole underneath where you plant the seeds (or seedlings, if you use transplants).

As for amounts, it's difficult to give a specific measure for something as bulky as composted manure, but a heaping shovelful for every 5 feet of row, or every hill, is usually fine. Or you can use a balanced commercial fertilizer, such as 5-10-10, at the rate of 2 Tablespoons for every hill, or 1 pound for every 25 feet of row.

Cover all fertilizers with 2 to 3 inches of soil to keep the seeds from being burned by the nitrogen in these substances.

By the way, the numbers on the labels of balanced commercial fertilizer refer to the percentages by weight of nitrogen (N), phosphate (P), and potash (K) contained in that particular mixture. They are always listed in the same order, N-P-K, for 5-10-10 or any other combination.

Vegetables need all three major nutrients: Nitrogen promotes leaf and vine production, phosphate builds strong roots, and potash conditions the entire plant. Nitrogen is probably most crucial for the vine crops, however.

PLANTING

Hills and Drills —
Simply Circles and Rows

Seed packets usually have planting instructions on the back, and you may be advised to plant vine crops in either hills or drills. These two terms have been used for years by gardeners and farmers to describe the planting arrangement of seeds, but it's much easier to picture these in terms of circles and rows.

When it comes to planting, a hill is not raised soil; it's a circle of four to eight seeds. A drill has nothing to do with your dentist; it's simply a row of seeds planted at regular intervals.

Contrary to the established tradition of planting vine crops in hills, you can also get good results by planting in rows, especially with the early-maturing cucumbers and summer squash. These plants don't run as much as some of the others, and you can fit many more plants in the same garden space by using rows.

Rows (Drills)

After preparing the soil and working it one last time on planting day, mark the row by stretching a string along the ground between two stakes.

Use a hoe to make a furrow beside the string. The depth of the furrow depends on your fertilizer. If you use a concentrated, granular, commercial fertilizer, the furrow has to be only 4 to 5 inches deep. If you have bulkier organic matter, such as manure or compost, just make a furrow that's 4 to 6 inches deep, then spread 2 to 3 inches of manure in it. Whichever fertilizer you use, cover it with 2 to 3 inches of soil so that the seeds are not in direct contact with the fertilizer.

Drop a seed every 6 to 8 inches in the row, depending on the variety.

Firm the seeds into the soil with the back of a hoe, creating good contact between seeds and soil; this is the key to good germination.

Cover the seeds with ¾ to 1 inch of soil.

Firm again.

Hills (Circles, Groups)

Planting techniques similar to planting in rows are used for hills. Mark the planting area with a string, but instead of making a furrow, dig a 4- to 8-inch hole for each hill, depending on the bulk of the fertilizer.

Space the holes 3 to 10 feet apart, depending on the vegetable.

Place either organic or balanced commercial fertilizer, such as 5-10-10, in the hole and fill it back to ground level. Be sure the fertilizer has at least a 2-inch soil covering.

Plant six to eight seeds on the perimeter of a circle at

each hill, allowing 2 to 3 inches between seeds. Drop each seed, firm, cover with soil, and firm again, just as in rows.

Later you'll thin each hill down to the best four to five plants. The extra seeds just ensure a full hill, even if germination is poor.

Mounds

It's important for vine crops that the soil be dry and warm. If your soil stays very wet and you've had trouble raising healthy vine crops, try building the hills up 3 to 5 inches before planting.

These mounds aid the plant's germination and improve the growing environment, because the soil warms up and dries out faster.

Vine Spacing

Generally, the longer it takes for vines to mature, the more they will spread. So, you should allow more room for winter squash and melons than for summer squash and cucumbers.

Here are some guidelines for seed and row spacing. It's a good idea to plant seeds closer together, just to insure good germination. It's easy to thin if there are too many young plants in a row or a hill; it's harder to patch up an incomplete row.

	Seeds in rows: inches apart	Transplants: inches apart	Rows or hills: feet apart
Cucumber	6 to 8	8 to 10	4 to 6
Summer squash	8 to 10	10 to 12	4 to 6
Winter squash	10 to 12	12 to 14	6 to 10
Pumpkins	10 to 12	12 to 14	6 to 10
Cantaloupe	6 to 8	8 to 10	4 to 6
Watermelon	6 to 8	10 to 12	6 to 8

To thin the rows or hills, allow the same spacing as for transplants.

Sprouting Tips

Melons are notoriously slow, undependable germinators. Here are a couple of tricks to give you germination insurance and a jump on the season. By the way, these methods work for all the vine crops.

PAPER TOWEL SPROUTING

Take four paper towels folded back into one and moisten them. Sprinkle about twelve seeds on the towel, about ¼ to ½ inch apart.

Roll the towel up tightly like a jelly roll, then roll the paper towel inside a soaking wet hand towel. Place the entire seed roll in a plastic bag, twist-tie the opening, and leave the bag in a warm spot where it can stay at an even temperature—the top of the refrigerator is usually a good spot. Just don't leave it on a windowsill, because the temperature there fluctuates too much.

The seeds will sprout in four to five days. Sometimes

all the seeds will sprout; sometimes only half or three-quarters. (You can also use this paper towel method to test the germination of any vegetable seeds. If you try to sprout ten seeds and only six germinate, the germination rate for that variety is 60 percent. This is a help if you have seed left over from the last season, and you want to know if it's still good.)

By the time the seeds have sprouted, have the garden soil prepared. You must plant seeds as soon as they sprout or they'll die.

These sprouted seeds are planted in exactly the same way as regular seeds. On the planting day, make the rows or hills and add fertilizer. Take the plastic bag out to the garden, unwrap and unroll it, and plant the seeds just as if they were unsprouted. Cover the seeds and firm as usual.

HOT CAPS

To gain two weeks on a short growing season, use inexpensive wax paper or plastic covers known as hot caps. They are designed to cover your seeds or seedlings, protect them from frost and some insects, and gather heat for them as they grow. Presprout the seeds and place hot caps over the seeds after you plant. When the danger of frost is past, remove the hot caps. The plants will be well up and on their way. Be sure to open the tops of the hot caps on sunny days so plants don't overheat.

Transplanting—Yes or No?

The choice of starting vine crops indoors or right in the garden is up to you. However, there are both advantages and disadvantages to transplanting vine crops that you should consider before you make up your mind.

Transplanting does give you a head start of a month or more on the growing season, and it protects the seeds and seedlings from birds, insects, heavy rains, sudden cold weather, and weeds.

On the other hand, starting seeds and transplanting seedlings is a time-consuming operation. It's also difficult to keep from injuring the sensitive roots when you transfer the plants into the garden.

To start your own vine crop plants indoors, follow these basic steps:

Choose disease-resistant seed from a reputable seed company.

Assemble your seeds, soil mix, and pots three to four weeks before the last frost date.

Use a separate container for each plant, rather than tubs or flats, so you won't disturb the roots during transplanting. You can use peat pots, pint milk cartons, or paper cups, so long as you punch a few holes in the bottom for drainage.

Moisten the soil thoroughly before planting the seeds.

Group the individual pots together on a tray, board, or rack, then slide the whole thing into a plastic bag to prevent drying. Top that with a few thicknesses of newspaper and place the pots in a warm spot that has an even temperature. Don't place it on a windowsill; the temperature changes there are too extreme.

When the seedlings first show, remove the plastic. Place the pots under fluorescent lights (no more than 5 inches away) or in a sunny spot to give them eight to fourteen hours of light—no more—each day.

Choose the healthiest, hardiest seedling from each pot after a week or so. Pinch off the other; pulling it out will disturb the roots of the one you're keeping.

Water the seedlings whenever the soil is very dry to the touch.

"Hardening Off"

You must gradually toughen young seedlings, or harden them off, so they won't get sunburned, windburned, or chilled after you transplant them. This is accomplished by exposing them to the elements little by little, until they're used to outdoor conditions.

Allow at least a week to ten days to harden your seedlings. When you start the process, don't water them for two days before you first bring them outside. From then on, water only when they really need it.

At first, place the seedlings in a sheltered spot away from wind and out of direct sunlight. Increase their exposure every day until they can tolerate a full eight to twelve hours of sun. Then leave them out overnight, unless there's a danger of frost. After two or three nights outside, they're ready for the garden.

Wise Shopping

If you buy transplants rather than raise them yourself, look for stocky, dark-green plants that aren't tall and spindly or leggy. The plants should be in individual containers. You must harden purchased transplants, too.

Some transplants come in peat pots of cardboard containers that have instructions telling you to plant the pots right along with the seedlings; they will decompose in the soil. We find that plants recover much better if these organic pots are gently peeled off at transplanting time without disturbing the soil around the roots. The roots then have immediate access to the food and moisture in the soil at a time when it really counts.

Sod Pots

Instead of planting in peat pots or other containers, you can use material from your own backyard—sod. Dig up a sod chunk 6 to 8 inches square and 2 inches thick. Turn it upside down and cut it in 2-inch cubes. Moisten the soil, then plant the seeds as you would in any container.

When the time comes to move the hardened seedlings into their permanent garden spot, prepare the furrows as usual, water the "sodlings," and place them in rows at the recommended intervals.

Transplanting How-to

Once it's warm enough and your seedlings are well hardened, you're ready to transplant them to a sunny garden spot.

First, soak the plants thoroughly. Moist dirt sticks to

the tender roots, protecting them from the elements and rough treatment.

Mark off the rows or hills in well-worked soil and make your holes or furrows. Always transplant seedlings into slightly deeper holes than their original containers.

Seedlings shouldn't be overfertilized, because they may grow too quickly and be too tender to survive the transplant shock. Fertilize sparingly and give them extra fertilizer (sidedress) later, when the plants are established. Cover the fertilizer with 2 to 3 inches of soil.

When everything is ready, take one seedling and plant it. Tilt the pot and tap the bottom to loosen the root ball. The whole plant will slip out into your hand. If you use peat pots, cautiously tear the outer skin of the pot away from the roots, being careful not to disturb them. If some of the pot sticks, leave it. You don't have to remove every last bit of peat, just enough so the roots aren't bound tightly on all sides.

Have some 2-inch newspaper squares on hand to wrap around the stems to prevent cutworm damage.

When transplanting, work quickly. Wrap a paper collar around the stem, so it spans 1 inch above to 1 inch below

the soil surface, where it keeps cutworms from chewing on the tender stem. Set the plant into the ground, cover the roots and part of the stem with soil, and firm the seedling into the soil to give the roots good contact with the soil.

Don't leave any of the seedling roots exposed to the air and light for more than a few seconds. If the phone rings when you're in the middle of this process, let it ring!

Water each plant thoroughly before going on to the next. Once the plants are in the ground, care for them just as you would plants started outdoors.

Trellising

Providing support for cucumbers and summer squash saves garden space. There are many kinds of homemade trellises. Let's just outline the ingredients for successful trellising:

The most sensible trellis is one that lasts, so keep this in mind before you start building.

You can make the support from wooden stakes and string, wooden slats nailed together to form a lattice, or chicken wire stretched between two posts. The vines climb easiest on crisscrossed materials that the tendrils can grab and wind around.

Unless you're interested in picking cucumbers from a ladder, keep the top of the trellis within easy reach, no more than 5 feet high.

Install your trellis on or before planting day. If you try to pound stakes into the ground later, you're bound to injure some roots.

If you have a choice, put your trellis on the prevailing downwind side of the plants. They'll lean into it on a windy day rather than being pulled away and possibly torn down.

Anchor the trellis solidly in the ground for the same reason.

Plant your seeds in rows on the prevailing upwind side of the trellis, and care for them just as you would free-growing plants.

When the plants are ready to run, guide them onto the supports. Wrap the tendrils or vines around the trellis to start them; they'll continue up on their own.

Stop the vines once they reach the top by picking off

the fuzzy tufts on the ends. There's no sense in allowing them to crawl down the other side, since they'd just get tangled up in the rest of the plant and you could end up with lots of too-small cucumbers.

One trellis caution is that since the plants are off the ground, they require more water. They "transpire," or lose moisture, more rapidly when they are exposed to warm air and drying winds, so you'll have to replenish the water supply fairly frequently. Mulching also helps to conserve moisture.

Babies' Bottoms

If you want to trellis any vegetables larger than cucumbers, you'll have to support each fruit, or the vines, tendrils, and stems will break from the weight.

Make a sling by tying both ends of a long, wide strip of cloth to your trellis—discarded pantyhose are perfect. Gently lift each fruit into its cradle.

It looks like a playpen full of diapered babies' bottoms when you're all finished, but it does save space and keeps the produce clean. Be sure to pick off the ends to control the growth of the vines.

Down with Fuzzies!

Once the vines take hold and start growing, you can expect to have lots of them sprawling over your garden —sometimes too many. This can be a problem, but there's a simple way to control it.

After the first fruits develop, pinch the fuzzy growth tips off the ends of the vines. These growth tips are the beginnings of the next leaf or vine extension. By keeping them picked, you interrupt the vine growth and prevent the vines from overrunning your garden.

You also cause the plant to direct its energy into ripening fruit rather than making longer vines. If you have a short growing season, or you're just impatient for that first melon or squash, picking the fuzzy vine ends can give you ripe fruit a week or so early.

New vines will shoot off in different directions once you start pruning the ends, but you can keep them in check with regular de-fuzzing.

Weed War

The most crucial time to control weeds is when the plants are young, before the vines start to run. Using a hoe, rake, or cultivating tool, stir up the top ¼ to ½ inch of soil around your plants at least once a week.

Don't cultivate deeper than this. Shallow cultivation won't injure the roots, and you'll expose the weed seeds just below the surface and get rid of them. You don't have to worry about deeper weed seeds; most only germinate if they're near the surface.

Once the vines start spreading, the broad leaves will shade out many weeds. You may have trouble picking your way through the network of vines, but do pull any tall weeds you see. You're bound to get weeds at the edges of the melon or squash patch where you've left room for the vines to travel. Rake or cultivate this area —1 to 2 inches deep—once a week before the vines reach it, and you'll diminish the weed problem.

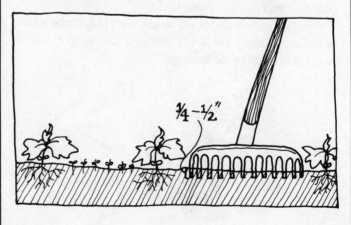

Mulching

One of the easiest weed controls of all, which also improves the growing environment (especially in the South), is mulch.

To mulch, you simply cover the ground around your plants with a layer of protective material (straw, hay, grass clippings, newsprint, black plastic). This shades the ground, making it impossible for most weeds to grow. Mulching also conserves moisture in the soil and, except for a few kinds such as roofing paper or black plastic, keeps the soil cool around the plants. This is especially important for southern gardeners, whose plants suffer in the scorching midsummer heat.

Wait until the soil has really warmed up before spreading mulch. Make sure it's 3 to 4 inches thick or it won't do its job effectively. As for newsprint, five or six thicknesses held down with stones will keep the garden weed-free.

Black Plastic

Black plastic is one mulch that keeps the soil warm, not cool, so it can really speed up vine crop growth in northern areas. Commercial growers use it with good results, and many gardeners praise it. The dark surface absorbs the heat of the sun and warms the soil beneath it.

Black plastic blocks out light, preventing weeds from growing beneath it, and it also conserves moisture because it eliminates evaporation. Water condenses on the plastic and drips back into the soil, so you don't need to water as often.

Lay the plastic down before you plant, making sure the soil is fairly moist. Cover the edges with dirt and rocks to anchor them securely. Cut round holes or crosses in the plastic, so plants can come up through them and water can go down.

Thinning

Young plants need room to develop a strong root structure and stem. If they are crowded, they will survive, but there may be too much competition.

If you plant six to eight seeds in each hill and they all come up, thin out all but the best four or five plants when they're a few inches high.

Plants in rows should be thinned to stand about 8 to 12 inches apart, depending on the variety. There's no trick to thinning these vegetables—just pull up the smaller, less healthy-looking plants, and leave the others.

Sidedressing

Sidedressing is simply applying a small amount of balanced commercial or organic fertilizer to a plant once it is four to five weeks old. It's called sidedressing because you place food a few inches to the side of the plant, where it will gradually seep down to the roots. This boost helps the plant speed up and increase production of high-quality fruit, and it's especially important for vine crops.

At one precise point in the plant's development, it seems to stand up very straight, to a height of 12 inches or more. That's the time to sidedress. The next time you see it, it will have flopped over and the vines will start to run or sprawl along the ground as they grow. At that point, the plant puts its energy into producing vines, blossoms, and fruit, and it can really use the extra food.

If you are using balanced commercial fertilizer, such as 5-10-10, make a shallow furrow down both sides of each row, or around each hill, about 4 to 5 inches away from the base of the plants.

Sprinkle the fertilizer evenly in the furrow—1 to 2 Tablespoons for each hill, or 1 pound per 25 feet of row. Cover the fertilizer with an inch or so of soil.

If you sidedress with bulky organic matter, such as manure, make the furrow deeper and a few inches farther from the plants. Spread the manure evenly in the furrow and cover it with an inch or two of soil.

Make it your golden rule to underfertilize if there's ever a doubt about how much to add. It's very easy to do your plants more harm than good with "one more handful just for good measure."

Water Wisdom

Vine crops are the camels of the garden! They contain up to 95 percent water at maturity, yet they don't require any more watering than other vegetables. What they *do* need is a steady supply of moisture—about an inch of water each week. A steady water supply is very important for taste, because cucumbers and melons can become bitter or bland if they are put under stress from dryness or lack of soil nutrients.

If you live in a fairly dry area, or if you experience a dry spell, you'll have to water. To make the most of your watering efforts, water when your plants need it, not just because you're in the habit of watering every seven days without fail. You can tell if your plants are thirsty by digging down into the soil. If the soil is dry 4 inches down, water. If you come upon moist soil around 3 inches down, your plants are okay. Remember this even if the top of the soil is bone-dry.

Another—and perhaps easier—way to tell if your plants need watering is if they look wilted before eleven o'clock in the morning. If your plants droop in the heat of the late afternoon sun, don't worry—that's normal.

How you water is just as important as when. Don't just sprinkle the soil surface to refresh the plants a little. Shallow watering promotes shallow, weak root growth, and that's bad for the plants. You should water to a depth of

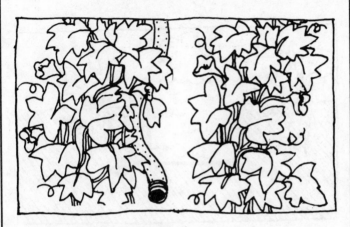

6 inches to do the most good.

You can water with an overhead sprinkler, a hose, or by bucket brigade. However, a soaker hose is the most efficient watering device for plants. It has tiny holes along its length, and by laying it right next to the plants, the water seeps out to soak the soil thoroughly. You don't wet the foliage, and hardly any water is lost to evaporation.

You can install a homemade "automatic" water dispenser. Punch a few holes in the bottoms of large, wide-mouthed cans or sawed-off plastic gallon jugs and bury these in the melon patch before planting. Plant seeds in hills around each can, about 4 inches from it. Rainwater will collect in the can and seep through the holes to the roots. Fill the cans when you water, and you'll make every drop go right to where it's needed.

Keep a careful eye on the weather and know your soil's water-holding capacity. With this knowledge, and with practicing good watering habits, you'll enjoy a bigger, better harvest.

Beware the WET Garden!

One of the best pieces of advice we can give you for the disease-prone vine crops is to stay out of the garden when it's wet. After a rain, in the morning when there's a heavy dew, or after you've just watered with a sprinkler, don't allow anyone in the garden. Diseases spread quickly if they can travel on beads of water from leaf to leaf or plant to plant, and even if you try not to touch the plants, you could transfer any number of disease-causing organisms without realizing it.

GOOD IDEAS DEPARTMENT

Lend-Lease Gardens

If you get discouraged at the thought of giving up garden space to vine crops and you don't want to worry about trellises or fences, save space—garden with a friend.

Get together with some of your neighbors and use just one garden for all the pumpkins and squash. Try this with other vegetables, too.

Chances are, there's a squash specialist among your gardening friends who would enjoy tending them in exchange for someone else growing the potatoes, beans, or something else. You would all save space and time with this communal/community garden.

Tin Can Alley

For sweeter melons, ripened weeks before any threat of frost, put these tips into practice in your garden.

Sprout the seeds before you plant, or start seedlings.

Plant two weeks early, under hot caps.

Start saving large tin cans. Coffee cans work well.

When the vines really start to take off, pick off the fuzzy vine ends to concentrate the plants' energy into producing flowers and fruit, rather than more vine.

When the melons start to form, partially bury the tin cans near them. The open ends should be placed downward, and the cans should be buried deep enough so they won't tip over.

When the melons are the size of baseballs, gently lift them onto the cans. The first sunlight of the day hits those cans and warms them, making the melons' day seem longer. The heat is transferred to the melons, and since they are sweetest if they ripen in hot weather, you'll have better-tasting melons. The raised melons are kept out of the shade of their foliage and in full sun off the cool ground.

Near the end of the summer, pick off all the little green melons you know don't have a chance of ripening before a frost. The remaining fruit will ripen faster and better.

The Champ

For some reason, vine crops—especially pumpkins and winter squash—seem to spark fierce and friendly competition among gardeners. The following tips should help you hold your own in the gardeners' game: "Top This!"

If you want to grow the biggest pumpkin on the block (or watermelon or squash), just follow these steps. But don't let any of the neighbors in on your growing secrets until harvest time.

Dig a hole and put in about a bushel of aged stable manure, or ¼ cup of 5-10-10 fertilizer, or some combination of the two. Then cover the fertilizer with about a five-inch layer of soil.

Select seeds that produce especially large fruit. For instance, *Big Max* is a favorite large pumpkin variety.

Plant three regular or presprouted seeds in the hill.

Cover the seeds with about an inch of soil and firm them into the soil.

When the seedlings have two or three leaves on them,

select the healthiest plant and remove the other two.

When the vine blossoms and produces its first three small melons, squash, or pumpkins, break off the vine's fuzzy end, so it won't grow any longer.

Pick off any new blossoms and fruit that appear, letting the plant feed only the original three.

When the fruits are about the size of your fist, again, select the best-shaped one and pick the other two. All the strength of the fertilizer will now go into just one fruit.

Roll the prize fruit over very gently once in a while. Changing its position helps it achieve a well-rounded shape with uniform color. Sidedress the plant a few times while the fruit is growing. The pumpkin, squash, or melon should grow to be a mammoth one.

All this pampering and pruning is to produce one prize fruit. The plant's energy will all be directed into developing one single giant.

This is a great project for kids. They will tend "The Giant Pumpkin" faithfully, just knowing it may grow to weigh more than they do!

Kids' Corner

CUKE-IN-A-BOTTLE

Create a natural conversation piece. When a cucumber first forms on a vine, slip it into a small-necked bottle or jar. Soon it will expand inside the jar, nearly filling it. Cut the vine, and bring the jar inside and put it on the kitchen table. The puzzled looks of friends are worth the small extra effort.

There are only two cautions about growing cukes in bottles. Keep checking the size of the cucumber, watching carefully that the glass doesn't break in the garden. And

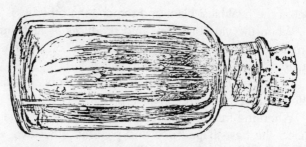

protect the bottle from the sun with a few sheets of newspaper; otherwise it will get too hot inside for the cuke.

GREAT IMPRESSIONS

Have a child sign his name and the date with a ball-point pen on any young melon, pumpkin, or winter squash. The letters will expand right along with the vegetable. Even really young kids love watching their names grow in the garden. Or, as a surprise, you can write their names for them. Later, when they see their names and ask how they got there, just say the seeds must have had their names on them.

JACK-O'-LANTERN TIPS

Halloween pumpkins really are a crop you should grow if you like kids. Come Halloween, jack-o'-lanterns are expensive to buy. A package or two of seeds will provide enough for the largest family, and even enough for a few friends.

If you have a pumpkin-carving party for kids—or even adults, for that matter—here are a few things to keep in mind:

Even though pumpkins may be oddly shaped, as long as they sit well, they'll make great jack-o'-lanterns.

The larger you cut the top, the easier it is to scoop out the goop and seeds from the inside. Save the seeds for the birds or for yourself. Roasted, they make a great snack.

Black marking pens, plenty of newspapers, sharp knives, and a good ghost-story teller are all you need for a good carving session.

JUST FOR FUN!

Gourds — Ornamental and Unusual

There are two basic types of ornamental gourds. The first are brightly colored, with fanciful shapes. Their names often describe them: apples, bells, pears, turbans, or eggs. You can grow them for table decorations, floral displays, and autumn harvest baskets.

In the second group, the gourds are more functional. Known as bottle- or dipper-shaped gourds, they, too, are used for decoration, but they can also be used as ladles (as they have been used in primitive cultures), jugs, planters, or even birdhouses.

In your garden, gourds are just like pumpkins, melons, or squash, except they require a longer growing season —140 to 150 days. Unless you live in an area that enjoys a long, hot summer, it's best to start the seeds indoors and transplant the seedlings after the last spring frost. Plant three or four seedlings in hills 6 to 8 feet apart, and care for them as you would any vine crop. Seedlings in rows should be 2 feet apart.

The vines of gourds really spread, so send them up a trellis or fence if you have one. This saves space, and it also gives you the best-shaped gourds. Also, a trellis draped with vines, blossoms, foliage, and colorful gourds makes a beautiful outdoor display or natural screen.

Harvest gourds when they are fully mature—when the shells are brightly colored, the skins hard, and the stems brown and dried. Don't use the fingernail test, because you'll ruin an unripe gourd if you break or dent the skin.

The larger, utensil-shaped gourds will tolerate light frosts, but the smaller, decorative ones will not. These should be harvested before the first frost. If they aren't quite ripe and an early frost is predicted, cover the plants for the night with a sheet or with newspapers. They'll probably survive the first frost, and chances are good that the next one will be a few weeks off.

Cut the gourds off the vine when stems begin to dry and turn brown, leaving a few inches of stem. Wash or wipe off any surface dirt, and dry the gourds for a week or two, being careful not to bruise them or let them touch one another. Then wash them in a Clorox solution (a cup of Clorox diluted in a gallon of water).

In another month, when they're completely dry, you can display the gourds just as they are, or you can wax, varnish, or paint their shells. Cut the long, bottle-shaped or crook-necked gourds into planter or birdhouse shapes, and enjoy their appearance while they serve a useful purpose.

Luffa, the Dishrag Gourd

Many specialty bath shops sell luffa sponges; these are usually grown commercially, but they are made from gourds you can grow at home. The seeds are available from companies that specialize in unusual vegetable varieties, and the plants require no more care than winter squash.

The plants grow quickly and will spread 10 to 15 feet. They need lots of water and sunshine, but if you live in a fairly temperate climate, you should be able to grow your own sponges with no problems.

For soft sponges, harvest the luffa gourds when they are 7 to 8 inches long; wait until they are larger for tougher scrubbers. The sponge part of the luffa is its fibrous inner layer. After drying the luffa gourd for a couple of weeks, simply peel the skin away to expose the interior, then leave it to dry for a week or so. When the pulp has dried, you can shake out the seeds. Then you can bleach the coarse sponge in the sun or in a mild solution of peroxide and water, and voilà: your own home-grown skin scrubber.

In some countries, the young luffa fruits are delicacies, served steamed or stir-fried, like pea pods.

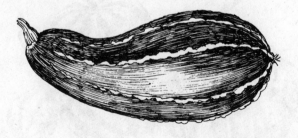

PROBLEMS

D Disease, Pest, and Insect Rx

Doctors tell you that the best way to fight disease is to prevent it. By making the effort to prevent problems, you don't have to worry so much about solving them.

How can you avoid trouble in the garden? First, buy disease-resistant seed varieties. Ask the extension agent in your area which diseases are likely to strike vine crops, and look for seeds bred to resist those diseases. Also, whenever possible, use treated seed to prevent rotting and damping off (a soil-borne disease that causes seedlings to fall over and die).

Keep you garden clean and weed-free during the growing season. This reduces the places in which disease-carrying organisms and insect populations can grow. Clean up all crop residues (vines, leaves, stalks, and discarded fruit) as soon as you finish harvesting. Till or spade this organic debris into the soil or add it to your compost pile to keep any harmful organisms from living through the winter and attacking next year's garden. Destroy any obviously diseased or infested plant debris.

Rotate your vegetables. Shift vine crops to different spots in the garden from one year to the next, and plant another vegetable family where those cucumbers or melons were. If you have a serious problem with any crop, don't plant it in the same place for two or three years.

Since several diseases that can plague vine crops are spread by cucumber beetles, protect your plants from them. To keep beetles from landing on your vine crops, start plants under hot caps or cloches, or spread a cheese-cloth covering over the row. You'll be way ahead in the battle against disease.

You can also use sprays or dusts to ward off garden diseases and insects. By checking with the extension service, you can be sure you are using the correct substance for your area and crop. Always read the instructions twice before applying any chemical sprays, following the directions carefully as you go. Read the instructions once again before you put the spray away, so that you store it safely.

Two final tips for a truly productive garden: (1) Test the pH of your soil every two years; the pH range should be between 6.0 and 6.8 for the best vegetable production. (2) Add plenty of organic matter to the soil each year; it helps to enrich it.

If you have any questions about a plant problem, contact your local cooperative extension agent. As the horticultural expert in your particular area, he or she can offer the most accurate diagnosis and solution.

Diseases

ANTHRACNOSE

Leaves will develop circular dark spots, vines may be streaked, fruit may develop dark sunken spots and drop off, and leaves may wither. Anthracnose thrives in humid weather. The fungus lives over the winter in seed and in refuse from diseased plants, and it can spread in splashing water. It affects cucumbers, muskmelons, and water-melons.

ANGULAR LEAF SPOT

Water-soaked spots develop on leaves, turn tan and gray, then drop out, leaving ragged holes. The spots on the fruit are rounded and may exude a thick, oozing substance. The infection will go into the seed cavity, making the fruit inedible. The bacterium lives over the winter in seed and plant debris, and is spread during wet weather. It affects cucumbers, pumpkins, and squash.

BACTERIAL WILT

The leaves of the plant wilt, then the entire runner, including any fruit, wilts. The affected area of the plant dries up and dies; eventually the entire plant will be killed. The disease is totally dependent on its host, the cucumber beetle, to survive the winter and be deposited on the young plants, so control the beetle to control the silt. It is most prevalent on cucumbers and muskmelons, but it does not affect watermelons.

To test for bacterial wilt, cut a stem and rub the two cut ends together. Pull them apart slowly. If a thick, gelatinous strand forms between them, the plant suffers from bacterial wilt.

FUSARIUM WILT

Causes damping-off of seedlings and stem blight; the vines may develop water-soaked streaks. Growth is stunted, leaves wilt, and the vines decay and die. It affects only muskmelons and watermelons. Fusarium lives from one season to the next on infected vines and builds up in the soil. Some seed is resistant to fusarium, which is indicted on the seed packet by "F."

POWDERY MILDEW

Thrives in warm weather. A gray-brown to white pow-derlike substance forms on the leaves and young stems. Foliage eventually dries up and dies.

DOWNY MILDEW

Shows up as irregularly shaped yellowish to brown spots on the tops of leaves; in moist weather, a purplish mildew may form on the undersides of these spots. Leaves die as the spots grow larger. It affects cucumbers and muskmelons, and it thrives in warm, wet weather.

MOSAIC VIRUS

Vines on virus-infected plants are stunted, leaves are mottled and dwarfed, and fruits may be oddly shaped, mottled, or bumpy. There's a different type of mosaic virus for each member of the vine crop family, referred to as cucumber mosaic virus (CMV), watermelon mosaic-2 (WM-2), and squash mosaic virus (SMV). Mosaic is carried by the cucumber beetle or by aphids if the virus has lived over the winter in perennial plants.

SCAB

Dry, corky spots develop on cucumbers and musk-melons. You can tell scab from angular leaf spot because scab shows a dark-olive-green velvety growth on the dis-ease spots. Spots can cover young stems and leaves, and the entire plant eventually dies. The disease thrives in foggy, cool weather and cool night temperatures.

If you notice a diseased vine or plant, cut or pull it right away. The remaining plants or vines may be perfectly healthy, so you may be able to keep the disease from spreading.

Some diseases can be controlled with fungicides; you can learn more about this from your local extension service. Your extension agent can help identify a disease and its treatment. In many cases, planting disease-resistant seed varieties, cleaning up crop residues, rotating your crops, staying out of the garden when it's wet, and keeping harmful bugs in check are the best ways to prevent disease.

Insects

CUCUMBER BEETLE

If you can control these striped or spotted pests in your garden, you'll go a long way toward preventing a diseased melon or cucumber crop. The most effective way to keep them in check is spraying: Starting when the plants first break through the ground, dust or spray with an approved pesticide. Be sure to treat the base of the plant, since beetles attack there. The beetles hatch four broods of eggs, so you have to repeat the spraying every five to seven days. Also, respray or dust after a rain, and don't forget the undersides of the leaves. Again, follow pesticide label instructions step-by-step, and check with your county extension agent if you have any questions.

APHIDS

These tiny, pear-shaped insects gather in colonies on the undersides of leaves. They can spread disease or destroy leaves and plants by sucking out the plants' juices. Spraying with an approved pesticide is the best way to beat them.

SQUASH VINE BORER

This pest is the larvae of a moth. It bores into stems

near the ground, causing plants to wilt and die. If you notice part of a vine wilting—the first sign of damage— you can perform a simple home remedy. Cut the stem lengthwise on one side where you see signs of boring,

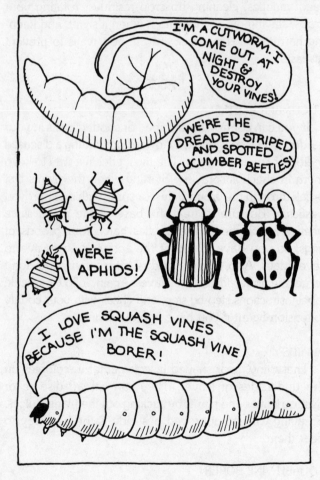

cut out the borer, then quickly cover the wounded stem with a mound of soil. The stem often recovers and continues growing. You can also apply an approved pesticide when adult moths are laying eggs in early summer.

CUTWORMS

These fat, hairless caterpillars can do incredible damage to young seedlings or transplants. They chew through the base of the stem, causing the whole plant to topple over and die. The best way to control cutworms in transplants is to wrap the stems with paper collars (newspaper strips are fine) that cover 1 inch below to 1 inch above the ground. For plants started outdoors, you can use an approved insecticide applied to the soil around the base of the plants.

SQUASH BUG

This flat, brownish-gray bug attacks squash by sucking the juices from the leaves. It lives over the winter in trash and garden residues, so a thorough clean-up helps prevent an infestation the following year. If squash bugs do show up in the garden, you can lay boards on the ground near the plants, where the bugs will gather at night. In the morning, you can lift the boards and destroy many bugs. You can also pick off any bugs or egg masses you see on the leaves (check the undersides, too). If you use an insecticide, be sure to spray on the top and bottom of the leaves—and follow directions carefully.

HARVEST TIME

Cukes and Summer Squash— You Deserve the Best

One of the wonderful things about having your own garden is that you have control over when you harvest your vegetables. You can pick them immediately before preparing them, ensuring that you have absolutely the freshest produce anywhere. But even better than that, you can also have the youngest. Most commercial growers don't pick tiny vegetables, knowing they'll get more for their money by waiting a few days. But the very best—especially cucumbers and summer squash—are the smallest. It may take six zucchini to make a meal—so what? There will be more—lots more—where they came from, so splurge. Treat yourself to the cream of the crop.

Be careful not to step on the vines when you harvest—you may kill the plants.

You may decide to let some cucumbers grow larger for pickles, or a crop might just get ahead of your harvest efforts—zucchini always seems to take off overnight. You can still eat these larger vegetables, although they won't taste quite as good as younger ones. Cucumber skins toughen as they mature, and summer squash loses some of its flavor. If the fruits grow big enough, the plant will stop producing. So even if you can't eat all of your harvest, keep the vines picked to encourage continued production.

If your vacation time coincides with the first harvest and you'll be away from home, make a deal with your neighbors. Ask them to keep the cucumbers and squashes picked, and let them keep all the produce. When you get back from your vacation trip, you'll be ready to reap your own harvest, your vines will still be producing, and you neighbors will be well stocked.

So, You're Overrun with Zucchini?

Most gardeners who plant zucchini end up with these long green vegetables coming out of their ears. Here's some practical advice on this matter:

Give it away—to friends, neighbors, relatives, strangers (perfect or not).

When you decide you've had enough zucchini, let one or two grow to be giants. The plant will stop producing. You can use the big ones in zucchini bread.

Melons

There is more than one way to judge a melon's ripeness, and most people learn from experience which is the most dependable method for them.

MUSKMELONS/CANTALOUPES

Smell: Check ripeness by smelling for a strong, "musky," or perfumey scent around the stem end of the melon. That unmistakable odor means ripeness every time.

Skin: When the skin color changes from green to yellow or tan and the netting becomes pronounced, the melon is ripe.

Stem: The stems on melons will separate or slip from the fruit with very little pressure as they start to ripen. A crack appears between the stem and the fruit, signaling the prime harvest time. When the stem finally separates completely, which is called full slip, the melon is very ripe and won't last long before turning all soft and mushy. Watch the slip signs and try to eat the ripest melon first to give yourself a steady supply of good ones.

Squeeze: Some people squeeze cantaloupes and assume a soft melon is ripe. This can be deceiving, since some harder melons may be ready to eat, too. So, save the squeezes and try other methods for judging melon ripeness.

WATERMELONS

Color: One of the signs of ripeness is the color of the spot where the watermelon rests on the ground. As the melon ripens, that "ground spot" turns from whitish to a deep, creamy yellow. Also, the shiny surface of the melon dulls somewhat when it's ripe.

Thumps: Unripe melons make a sharp ringing sound when rapped and ripe ones sound muffled. But overripe melons make that same dead sound, so this isn't the most reliable test.

Curly-cues: Gardeners sometimes watch the watermelon stem to judge ripeness. When the tendril nearest the stem turns brown and dries up like a curly pig's tail, the melon's ripe. But, some varieties may show this sign and not ripen for another week or so, so you could easily be disappointed.

However you judge your cantaloupes and watermelons for ripeness, if you cut into them and find juicy, deep orange or red flesh, you can be confident you know how to pick 'em!

Winter Squash and Pumpkins—Thumbs Up!

First, you should know that you don't have to worry about these vegetables going by before harvest time. The seeds inside them won't grow large enough to trigger the plant's stop-production mechanism until there's plenty of fruit already on the vines. Wait until all vines die or until just before the first hard frost to harvest your winter squash and pumpkins.

The signs of ripeness are simple. If your thumbnail can't penetrate the vegetable's skin, it's fully mature, long-lasting, and a good keeper in storage.

It may help first to check the vegetables for a deepening of their skin color before you stick your nail into them. If you test one and your thumbnail breaks the skin, use it right away, because it won't store very long.

Most of the winter squashes or pumpkins on each plant should be ripe about the same time. Harvest those you intend to store on a sunny day, after a few days of dry weather, if possible.

Cut them off the vines, leaving some stem on each. Roll them over and leave them outside for a few hours until the dirt and earthworms on the underside dry out and drop off.

Be careful not to bruise vegetables you want to store —they won't keep well. Don't carry them by the stems; stems won't support the weight, and a broken stem is an entryway for rot organisms.

You can wash winter squash and pumpkins with a bleach solution to kill bacteria on the skin. This helps the vegetables keep longer and better. Sponge off with or dip the vegetables in a cup of Clorox diluted in a gallon of water. Drip dry and don't rinse.

B Winter Keep—Not for All

ack when winter keep, or common storage, was the only way to extend the harvest past the first killing frost, winter squashes were a household staple because of their good keeping qualities. They still keep best if stored properly in a cool, dry, dark spot, and they don't need any fancy rooms or equipment. Pumpkins also store well for months at a time.

The rest of the vine crops have to be pickled, canned, or frozen if you want them to last, although some honeydew melons and large zucchini will keep for a while.

Curing

Pumpkins and all winter squashes (except for acorn squashes) must be cured in order to dry and harden their shells completely before they are put into storage. Ideally, they should be aired out in a warm, well-ventilated place at a temperature of 75° to 85°F for a week or two. It's usually too cool at harvest time to achieve the perfect temperature, but you can group the vegetables near your furnace, wood stove, or on a sunny back porch, where they can be sufficiently cured.

Storing

After curing, store squashes and pumpkins in a warm (50°–60°F), dry spot. Acorn squashes are the exception —store them at 32° to 40°F. In the past, people stashed their winter squash and pumpkins under their beds. Unless your bedroom is unheated and your bed is high enough, this is not practical today. But any cool, dry, dark spot is fine—a spare room, closet floor, attic floor, basement rafters, or even in a large, cool kitchen cupboard.

Wherever you store the produce, check regularly and take out any that are getting soft or look as if they're starting to rot. It's only natural that some will keep better than others.

If a squash has started to soften, cook it plain, without butter or seasonings, and freeze it in containers.

And don't worry about the soft spots. Just cut them out and eat the rest. It's perfectly good.

GARDEN TO KITCHEN

Preparing and Storing Squash

SUMMER SQUASH

To prepare summer squash (Yellow Straight-neck and Crookneck, Zucchini and Patty Pan), wash the whole vegetable, trim off the ends, and cut into half-inch cubes or slices. Serve raw, unpeeled, thin slices in salads or with dips. Cook slices over steam or in a small amount of boiling water until just tender. Do not overcook. Three to five minutes should do it. Add butter, lemon juice, herbs, or spices, and serve hot.

To steam winter squash, place pieces in a blancher, basket, or colander over boiling water until tender, about thirty minutes. Scoop out cooked pulp, and mash or puree the squash in a blender or food mill. Use the cooked squash in recipes, or freeze for later use. Pumpkin can be steamed or baked the same way.

You can flavor baked winter squash with spices and butter, honey, maple syrup, or brown sugar. Serve cooked squash as is, or combine it with other ingredients for pies, soups, or cookies.

Other than root cellar storage, freezing is a good way to keep winter squash. Just fill freezer containers with precooked, cooled, mashed squash. Then label the containers with the date and contents, and freeze them. To freeze uncooked winter squash, peel and cube it, blanch it for three minutes, cool, drain, pack it in containers, and freeze.

For best results, freeze baked or steamed squash, rather than boiled. Because it's somewhat drier, it is the right consistency for casseroles, cookies, and pies.

To reheat frozen winter squash, place it in the top of a double boiler over medium heat with water boiling in the lower pot, stirring occasionally until it's thoroughly defrosted. Or, place each pint of frozen squash in ½ cup boiling, salted water and simmer for ten minutes, or until heated through.

A note on canning: We generally don't recommend canning any summer squash, winter squash, or pumpkins. These vegetables all require steam pressure canning, and canned squash tends to be mushy and flavorless when reheated. We think you'll have better luck with freezing and root cellar storage.

SPAGHETTI SQUASH

This unusual squash is quickly becoming a favorite among home gardeners, adding a new dimension to Italian-style dishes. It grows just like any winter squash and should be harvested when it's fully ripe—when the rind turns completely yellow.

The crisp, spaghettilike strands of this unusual squash can be used in all your recipes that call for macaroni, noodles, or spaghetti.

To cook, wash the squash, prick the skin, and bake it whole in the oven (350°F) for about one hour—until the skin is fork-tender, or soft to the touch. You can also boil the whole squash for about thirty minutes, until tender. If the squash is very large, cut it in half using a sharp knife. Scoop out the seeds and cook only as much as you want to use. Refrigerate the rest.

After the squash is cooked, cool it slightly. Split whole squash in half lengthwise and remove the seeds and membrane. Gently lift the meaty squash strands from the shell with a fork, or simply fluff up the strands and serve the squash right in the shell.

This is delicious served simply with butter, pepper, and salt. Or you can add parsley, grated cheese, or your favorite spaghetti sauce. The strands of squash can be layered in a casserole with sauce and cheese and baked like lasagna. One medium squash serves four.

Ripe vegetable spaghetti will store just like winter squash, and two plants will yield enough fruit to feed four people all summer.

Pickling

Pickling is one of the easiest and oldest ways to preserve food, since it uses very little energy or special equipment. You simply ferment vegetables (or meat) in a salt brine or vinegar solution, and store them until the process is complete. Pickling is about the only way to keep cucumbers once the harvest is over.

You can pickle in two ways. Either ferment vegetables in brine for many weeks, or fresh-pack the produce in a vinegar solution in Mason jars, seal them using a boiling water bath, and let them ferment in the jars for four to six weeks.

The fresh-pack method is quick and easy, and you can prepare just a few jars or a large batch of cucumbers when they're just ready for pickling. Whether you use a fresh-pack recipe or a pickling crock to ferment vegetables, your goal is tasty, crisp pickles that will keep indefinitely.

To ferment in a salt brine, use stone crocks or kegs, or clean, watertight, hardwood barrels that are lined with enamel, glass, or paraffin. Although pickles will keep fairly well stored in such containers, for safety reasons we urge you to transfer fermented pickles to canning jars and process them for storage.

Use special pickling or dual-purpose cucumbers that grow no longer than 2½ to 4 inches. Their small size and thin skins make them ideal for curing. Prepare the freshest, cleanest produce for pickling, and try to use vegetables that are slightly underripe. Wash vegetables well, remove the end blossoms, then follow your favorite recipe.

The key to crisp pickles is to use only fresh, just-harvested produce. Even if you store vegetables in the refrigerator, you lose quality with each hour that passes after they've been picked. Also, work quickly once you start the pickling process, so the pickles will ferment uniformly.

The ingredients you use for the pickling brine are very important to ensure crisp, flavorful, evenly cured vegetables.

Salt: Use only pure, granulated salt with no noncaking material or iodine added. This is sold as pickling salt, barrel salt, and kosher salt. Table salt and iodized salt contain materials that may interfere with fermentation, darken the pickles, or cloud the pickle juice.

Vinegar: Use a 4-to-6-percent acidity cider or white vinegar. If the label doesn't have the acidity listed, don't use it for pickles or relishes. Never use less vinegar than the recipe specifies, since the amount of acidity is crucial to safe processing.

Water: Soft water is best for pickling. You can soften hard water by boiling it, skimming off the surface scum, and letting it sit for twenty-four hours. Don't disturb the sediment at the bottom when you use this softened water.

Alum: It used to be essential for crispness, but if the proper ingredients are used, alum isn't needed. If you use alum, don't use it to excess—it can irritate the digestive system.

BOILING WATER BATH CANNING
Note: This method is for pickles only! Summer and winter squash must be canned under pressure.

Once you have all your vegetables and pickling ingredients ready, use either the fresh-pack method or a salt-brine fermentation. Then follow these steps for the boiling water bath canning. If your canner instructions vary from

these, follow the instructions that came with your canner.

Assemble all utensils: Canner with rack, Mason jars, lids, tongs or jar lifter, cooling racks, and nonmetallic spatula.

Use only Mason jars for home canning. They are made by a number of manufacturers and are safe because the glass is heat-tempered and can seal perfectly.

Never reuse dome lids for canning. The rubber compound loses its ability to seal perfectly after one use. Metal screw bands and Mason jars may be reused.

Examine and clean all equipment: Check all bands for rust, dents, or nicks, and the jars for chips or cracks. Don't use them for canning if they are not perfect.

Wash all equipment in hot, soapy water. Rinse in clear, hot water. Keep jars and screw tops hot. Keep dome lids in hot water until ready to use.

Follow recipe instructions for filling jars, always leaving

¼ inch headspace for pickles.

Once jars are filled, release all air bubbles from jar by running a plastic or rubber spatula down around the inside of the jar. Wipe jar top and threads clean with damp cloth. Put lid on jar, rubber side down, and screw band on firmly.

Fill the canner half full with hot water. Place the rack on bottom of canner. Only fill as many jars as the canner will hold in one batch. As each jar is filled, place it in the rack. The jars should not touch each other or the side of the canner.

Add hot water, if necessary, so the jars are covered with at least 1 to 2 inches of water. Cover and turn up heat under canner. Start timing when the water reaches a rolling boil. Follow timing instructions for each recipe.

To complete the processing, use jar lifter or tongs to remove the jars and put them upright on a rack or thick towel in a draft-free area, allowing enough room between jars so air can circulate.

Do not tighten the metal rims, because you may break the seals.

After twelve hours of cooling, test the seals. There are three tests recommended for checking the seals on dome lids:

1. As the jar contents cool and the vacuum forms, the lid pulls down into the jar and makes a "kerplunking" sound.
2. The lid will be concave or dished and should stay that way as long as the vacuum is present—you can feel it.

3. Push down on the lid with your thumb. If it doesn't push down, the jar is sealed. If it makes a clicking sound, the seal isn't complete.

If you have some jars with incomplete seals, reprocess the contents, using a new lid and a clean jar. Or, if the contents have already been fermented, simply put the jars in the refrigerator and use the pickles soon.

Wipe the jars with a clean, damp cloth, label clearly, and store. The outer rims should be removed, because moisture can build up under these and affect the lids and seals on the jars. Store jars in a cool, dry, dark place.

Don't open the jars for several weeks—this will allow the flavors of the herbs and spices to develop fully.

Before serving, check pickles or relishes for signs of spoilage, sliminess, softness, frothing, or foul odor. Don't eat any pickles you think are bad—don't even taste them. Throw them out if there's the slightest doubt as to whether they're good.

GREEN MOUNTAIN CUCUMBERS

Here's a new way to serve cucumbers. Even heated, they stay crisp and delicious. Serve with fish or a cold meat platter.

- 4 **medium cucumbers**
- 4 **Tbsp butter or margarine**
- 1 **clove garlic, crushed**
- 1 **cup sour cream**
- ½ **tsp salt**
- ¼ **tsp pepper**
- 1 **Tbsp chopped fresh dill weed**
- 1 **Tbsp chopped fresh chives**
  parsley sprigs

Peel cucumbers, cut in half lengthwise, scoop out seeds, and cut in ½-inch slices.

Heat margarine in large skillet. Add garlic and cucumbers. Sauté, stirring often, for five minutes.

Add sour cream, salt, and pepper. Cook, stirring constantly, over medium heat for five minutes; do not boil, or sour cream will separate. Stir in dill and chives. Heat one minute. Garnish with sprigs of parsley. Serves 6.

DILL PICKLES

*S*tart *harvesting batches of tiny cukes for dill pickles when they are only 2 to 3 inches long. Even so, they grow so fast that they tend to get ahead of you. Plant your dill early to be sure it's in bloom when pickling time arrives.*

Put up a lot of these because family, relatives, and friends love them.

Per quart jar:
1 Tbsp salt
1 tsp mustard seed
1 small piece alum (size of a small grape)
2 heads fresh dill or 1 Tbsp dill weed
1 cup vinegar
2 cups water

Wash quart jars. In each jar put salt, mustard seed, alum, and dill.

Sort the cucumbers according to size and put similar-sized cukes in each jar, so they pickle uniformly. Use only small cucumbers or spears. Fill to an inch from top of jar.

Measure vinegar and water for each filled jar and heat to boiling. Pour hot liquid into jars, leaving ¼ inch headspace. Adjust lids and process ten minutes in hot water bath.

SUNSHINE PICKLES

The turmeric makes these pickles a bright, "sunshine" yellow.

    4 quarts ripe cucumbers, cut in small chunks
    4 large onions, sliced
    1 Tbsp salt
    1 Tbsp celery seed
    1 Tbsp turmeric powder
    4 cups sugar
 2½ cups vinegar
  ½ cup water

Cook all ingredients until cucumbers are fork-tender. Put in jars, leaving ¼ inch headspace, adjust lids, and process in hot water bath for ten minutes.

ICICLE PICKLES

We recommend processing these crock-cured pickles in a boiling water bath for long-term storage.

Fill 1-gallon crock with good-quality, green, solid cucumber spears. Mix ½ pound of canning salt in enough boiling water to cover spears. Cover them with a weighted-down plate or lid.

Let stand one week. Drain thoroughly. Add two pieces of alum, each about the size of a grape, or 2 Tbsp powdered alum, to enough boiling water to cover the cukes. Let stand twenty-four hours and drain well.

Mix 5 cups vinegar, 5 cups sugar, and 1 small handful pickling spice (in mesh bag). Bring to a boil and pour over pickles. Let stand twenty-four hours, then drain again, saving the syrup. Repeat this procedure once a day for four days, bringing the syrup to a boil each time.

On the fifth day, or any time thereafter, put pickles in canning jars and add hot liquid to fill jars, leaving ½ inch headspace. Seal and process in a boiling water bath for ten minutes.

Large batches are easy to make. Use a larger crock, with proportionately more cucumbers and other ingredients. A little simple arithmetic—depending on the size of the crock—and you'll have it.

WATERMELON RIND PICKLES

This is a great way to use the rinds of watermelons after a summer picnic or family gathering. Enjoy the watermelon, but save the rinds.

8 cups watermelon rind (1 large watermelon)
½ cup salt
2 quarts water
2 cups vinegar
3 cups white or brown sugar
1 lemon, sliced thin
1 stick cinnamon
1 tsp allspice
1 tsp whole cloves

Remove skin and pink from rind. Cut rind into 1-inch cubes or chunks. Soak chunks overnight in brine mixture of ½ cup salt and 2 quarts water. Drain and rinse in fresh water. Drain again. Add more fresh water to cover, and simmer until tender. Make syrup of vinegar, brown sugar, lemon, and spices. Simmer five minutes. Add rind and cook until clear. Pack rinds into hot jars and fill with syrup, leaving ½ inch headspace. Adjust lids and process in hot water bath for ten minutes.

MELONS

Use melons cut in wedges, plain or with a squeeze of fresh lime and mint leaf. For dessert, top melon wedges with scoops of ice cream or sherbet, or serve sliced cheddar cheese alongside.

When the harvest is really overflowing, scoop out the melons with a melon baller, serve plenty of fruit cocktails or compotes, and freeze what you can't eat right away.

To freeze melon balls, slices, or cubes, use only firm, ripe fruit. Cut melon in half, remove any seeds, and cut out fruit. Don't cut into any of the rind.

You can place melon directly in containers: label, date, and freeze. But if you want the melon pieces to keep their shape, place them on a cookie sheet and place in freezer overnight (six to twelve hours). Transfer frozen fruit to plastic freezer bags or containers. Seal, label, and date. Return to freezer and use as needed. Melons, if properly frozen, will keep up to a year in your home freezer. Frozen melon balls taste best if served while still slightly frozen.

Cantaloupes and watermelons really spruce up a summer meal when you scoop out the fruit and fill them with a cold combination salad. You can carve scalloped, pointed, fluted, or zigzagged edges. Be creative!

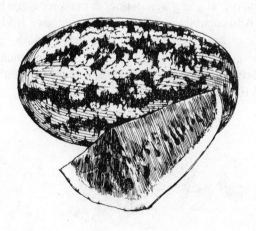

SUMMER SQUASH MEDLEY

This is best made with garden-fresh vegetables, but in winter you can use stored vegetables. Or make big batches when these vegetables are abundant and freeze for later use. These ingredients are approximate.

¼ cup chopped onion
¼ cup chopped green pepper
2 Tbsp margarine
2 cups peeled and cubed eggplant (1-inch cubes)
2 small (4- to 6-inch) squashes, cut in 1-inch cubes
2 cups chopped tomatoes
¼ cup stuffing mix or herbed bread crumbs
½ cup grated cheddar cheese

Sauté onion and green pepper in margarine in a heavy skillet. Add vegetables and simmer until tender. Add stuffing mix or bread crumbs and mix well. Sprinkle grated cheese on top, cover, and heat until cheese melts. Or slide dish under broiler until cheese melts and bubbles. Serves 6 to 8.

FRENCH-FRIED ZUCCHINI

Here's a nice change from potatoes that kids (and grown-ups) really go for. It's so easy.

 2 **medium zucchini, cut in ½-inch julienne strips**
   (2 cups)
   salt and pepper to taste
 2 **eggs, well beaten**
 ½ **cup flour**
 ½ **cup bread crumbs**
   hot salad oil or shortening

Sprinkle squash slices with salt and pepper. Dip into egg, dredge in flour, then dredge in bread crumbs. Fry in deep fat until golden brown. Or fry in skillet in hot oil, turning once. Drain on paper towels, serve hot. Serves 4.

PLEASE, DO EAT THE BLOSSOMS

Squash blossoms are a real taste adventure, either fried (in the batter above or your favorite frying batter) or sautéed. Pick a dozen or so blossoms when they're in full bloom, leaving enough male flowers on the vine for pollination. Wash blossoms and remove stems.

To sauté, melt butter or margarine in a heavy skillet and cook blossoms until heated through.

This used to be an Italian specialty, but more and more gardeners are discovering how tasty the blossoms can be.

BAKED STUFFED ZUCCHINI

This is a good way to use zucchini that have hidden under the leaves and become too big.

4 zucchini, 6 inches long (or 2 large, 10- to 12-inch zucchini)
½ cup soft bread crumbs
1 egg, beaten
½ cup grated cheese, cheddar or Parmesan
¼ cup chopped onion
1 clove garlic, minced
2 Tbsp margarine or butter
1 lb ground beef or hot sausage
½ tsp salt
⅛ tsp black pepper
3 Tbsp grated cheese

Wash zucchini and trim ends. Simmer in boiling, salted water until just tender—about ten minutes. Cut in half lengthwise. Remove seeds and stringy center. Scoop out squash and combine it with bread crumbs, egg, and cheese. Drain zucchini shells upside down on paper towel.

Sauté onion and garlic in margarine. Brown ground beef separately. Combine onion, garlic, and beef with bread mixture.

Fill zucchini shells with mixture and top with extra cheese. Bake in greased baking pan in 350°F oven for thirty-five to forty-five minutes, until brown. Serves 8. Can be served for dinner with broiled tomatoes or green salad.

SQUASH AND APPLE CASSEROLE

*T*his goes well with any meat dish, and can double as a dessert!

1 medium winter squash (butternut or acorn is best; the flesh stays firm)
½ cup maple syrup or packed brown sugar
¼ cup margarine, melted
1 Tbsp flour
½ tsp salt
½ tsp nutmeg
3 cups sliced apples (peel if desired)
¼ cup chopped nuts

Wash squash, cut in half lengthwise, take out seeds, peel, and cut in small chunks. Stir sugar or syrup, margarine, flour, salt, and nutmeg together.

Arrange squash in an ungreased rectangular baking dish. Place apple slices on top. Sprinkle sugar/flour mixture and nuts over apples. Cover with foil. Bake in 350°F oven for fifty minutes or until squash is tender. Serves 4.

Variation: Bake acorn squash halves at 350°F for thirty-five minutes. Fill centers with apples, top with sugar mixture and nuts. Cover with foil and bake about twenty-five minutes more, until squash is tender. Sprinkle with cinnamon, if desired.

WINTER SQUASH SOUP

2 lbs winter squash
1 cup water
1 tsp salt
1 cup chopped onion
½ small clove garlic, minced
2 Tbsp butter
2 cups milk
2 cups light cream
½ cup medium-dry sherry
  salt and pepper to taste
  toasted sliced almonds

Peel, seed, and dice squash. Combine with water and 1 tsp salt in saucepan. Bring to a boil and simmer, covered, until squash is very tender.

Meanwhile, sauté onion and garlic in butter until tender. Add squash to onions, then add milk and cream and liquefy mixture in blender. Add sherry and salt and pepper to taste. Heat to serving temperature. Serve garnished with toasted almonds. Serves 6 to 8.

About the
National Gardening Association

The National Gardening Association is a nonprofit member-supported organization dedicated to helping people be successful gardeners at home, in community groups, and in institutions. We believe gardening adds joy and health to living, while improving the environment and encouraging an appreciation for the proper stewardship of the earth.

Established in 1972, this national organization of 250,000 members is now the premier membership organization for gardeners.

Members receive the monthly *National Gardening* magazine, may write the staff horticulturist for help with any gardening problem, receive discounts on gardening books, and get other member benefits. *National Gardening* magazine provides in-depth, how-to articles, profiles of members and their gardens, and evaluations of garden tools and products. Regional articles help members with special climate challenges. The magazine also provides a forum for NGA members in a "Seed Swap" exchange column, and seed and recipe search columns.

The National Gardening Association is a nationwide resource for information, services, and publications related to gardening. Besides the monthly magazine, NGA produces numerous books and directories for the home gardener. NGA also produces the annual *National Gardening Survey*, from research conducted for NGA by the Gallup Organization. This comprehensive report on trends in home gardening in America is widely used by the lawn and garden industry and is cited by the nation's media.

Well known as the information clearinghouse for community garden programs across the country, NGA offers on-site planning assistance, specialized manuals, a network to other organizations, and the annual National Gardening Grant Program—for gardens in neighborhoods, schools, and institutions, especially garden groups for youth, senior citizens, and people with disabilities.

The National Gardening Association continues to explore new ways to gather and share information, to connect gardeners with other gardeners, and to further its mission—successful gardeners everywhere!

If you would like a free sample issue of the *National Gardening* magazine and information on member benefits and how to join the National Gardening Association, please write or call:

The National Gardening Association
180 Flynn Avenue
Burlington, Vermont 05401
(802) 863-1308

Villard's National Gardening Association Series

75000-4 ☐ **BOOK OF TOMATOES**	$4.95; in Canada, $7.50
74991-X ☐ **BOOK OF LETTUCE & GREENS**	$4.95; in Canada, $7.50
74990-1 ☐ **BOOK OF EGGPLANT, OKRA & PEPPERS**	$4.95; in Canada, $7.50
74988-X ☐ **BOOK OF CUCUMBERS, MELONS & SQUASH**	$4.95; in Canada, $7.50

To order, send check or money order (no cash or CODs) to:

Villard Books, c/o Random House, Inc., 400 Hahn Road, Westminster, MD 21157

Please enclose $1.00 for the first book and 50¢ for each additional book to cover postage and handling. Make checks payable to Villard Books. If you have a major credit card, you can charge by phone by calling:

(800) 638-6460

You may also charge to your credit card by mailing in this coupon.

Please send me the books I have checked above.

NAME (please print)

ADDRESS

CITY/STATE   ZIP

PLEASE CHECK ONE: MASTERCARD ☐   VISA ☐

AMERICAN EXPRESS ☐

CARD NUMBER

EXPIRATION DATE

SIGNATURE

Please add applicable sales tax. Allow 4–6 weeks for delivery.